Total Consecration to Mary

Nine-day Preparation in the Spirit of
St. Maximilian Kolbe

Fr. Anselm Romb, OFM CONV.

Theology and History of Marian Consecration by
Fr. Patrick Greenough, OFM CONV.

Marytown Press
1600 West Park Avenue
Libertyville, Illinois 60048
847-367-7800

MI International Center:
www.mi-international.org

MI National Center, U.S.A.
Marytown
1600 W. Park Avenue
Libertyville, IL 60048
847-367-7800
www.consecration.com

MI Youth National Office, U.S.A.
209-743-2314
www.miyouth.org

Milicia de La Inmaculada MI Spanish
Fr. Kolbe Missionaries of the Immaculata
531 E. Merced Ave.
West Covina, CA 91790
626-917-0040
www.kolbemission.org

MI Canada
1099 Danforth Avenue
Toronto, ON Canada M4J 1M5
209-743-2314

ISBN: 0-913382-13-2
MP 105-37

First Edition 1983
Second printing 1986
Second Edition 2000
Third Edition 2004
Fourth Printing 2006

© 2006, Marytown Press, 1600 W. Park Ave., Libertyville, IL 60048.
847-367-7800. All rights reserved. Printed in the U.S.A.

Contents

Preface 4

The Theology and History of Marian Consecration 6

Introduction 23

DAY ONE: Mary, Spouse of the Holy Spirit 27

DAY TWO: Mary's Humble Dependence on God 33

DAY THREE: Mary, the Virgin Mother 38

DAY FOUR: Mary Joins Herself to Jesus 43

DAY FIVE: Mary, Our Model of Spirituality 48

DAY SIX: Mary Leads Us to Obey Christ 55

DAY SEVEN: Mary, the New Eve 60

DAY EIGHT: Mary, Model of Faith 65

DAY NINE: Jesus Entrusts His Disciples to Mary 69

A Chronology of St. Maximilian Kolbe, OFM CONV. 74

Catechism on the Militia of the Immaculata 78

Ritual for Consecration in the Militia of the Immaculata 89

Preface

If you do not want your life to change *do not* consecrate yourself to the Virgin Mary. She will take you at your word and use you for whatever and whenever she needs you. In other words, your life will never be the same! I do not regret a single day of my consecration.

All consecrations, however, are to God and by God. It is God who inspires us, who plants the seeds of desire to consecrate ourselves to Him. We are merely responding to God's call. All consecration is also to God. While we speak of consecrating ourselves to the Virgin Mary, we are in the end really being consecrated to God, with Mary and through Mary. All consecrations, therefore, are directed to God and end in God.

The ultimate and most important consecration is Baptism. All of our other consecrations flow from our baptism and return to our baptism to help us live our baptismal promises more perfectly and deeply. Through Baptism all sin (original and personal) is removed and the divine life of God is poured into our souls. At our baptism we promise to remain faithful and to turn away from sin. If we do this, God promises us eternal life. Our consecration to Mary helps us to live our baptismal consecration more perfectly.

The reason we consecrate ourselves to Mary is that no one lived their consecration more perfectly than Mary. She was consecrated *by* God to be the Mother of His only Son, and was consecrated *to* God, set apart from the world to live for God alone. Mary, therefore, is the perfect model and guide for us to live our consecration and that is why

Christ himself entrusted her to us as our Mother at the foot of the Cross, to teach all of her children, as a mother does, how to live their consecration.

You can entrust/consecrate yourself confidently to Mary knowing that the Son of God entrusted/consecrated himself to her womb and entrusted/consecrated us to her from His Cross.

May this small book be just the beginning of a deeper life of holiness and love in the Most Holy Trinity through the Daughter, Mother, and Spouse of the Father, Son and Holy Spirit, now and forever.

—Fr. Patrick Greenough, OFM CONV.
National President of the Militia of the Immaculata

The Theology and History of Marian Consecration

What Is Consecration?

1. Consecration in the proper sense is to God and by God, for He alone can divinize, make us in His image and likeness by means of His divine grace.

2. The true and ultimate Christian consecration is Baptism, which God gives to us without any merit on our part. Baptism is the beginning of our Christian life whereby God pours His divine life into us.

3. God does not do anything in us or to us without us. It is necessary therefore, that we give ourselves to God and that we ask for consecration.

4. The total giving of oneself in Baptism cannot be better accomplished than by consecrating oneself through Mary.

5. Through consecration, therefore, we unite ourselves with Mary and imitate her who responded to the Will of God in all things, and who was the perfect instrument of the Holy Spirit and the disciple par excellence of Christ.

Why the Virgin Mary?

Many people ask the question, "Why do I have to go through Mary?" The answer to such a question is, "You do not have to! God does not force us to do anything." The real question that should be asked is, "Why do I want to go through Mary?"

The following short treatise on the history and theology of consecration shows why people from the beginning of Christianity have chosen to go through Mary. Our mission as members of the MI who are consecrated to Mary is to share with others why we have chosen to go to Christ through Mary and how it has changed our lives, strengthened our faith and made us more perfect disciples of Christ.

Consecration is a Relationship

Consecration to the Virgin Mary is essentially a relationship with her. This relationship has been expressed in many different ways throughout the ages by many different people. While some of the saints, therefore, did not use the word consecration in their writings, their relationship with the Virgin was for all intents and purposes identical with what takes place in consecration, namely a total giving of oneself, and entrusting of oneself to Mary as their Mother, Queen, Mediatrix and Advocate. St. Francis of Assisi never used the word consecration in his writings, but his relationship with the Virgin Mary was similar to that of St. Maximilian Kolbe of entrusting oneself totally to her.

Characteristics of the Militia of the Immaculata

1. Historical: The MI is an historical movement that begun on October 16, 1917 by St. Maximilian Kolbe and six other Conventual Franciscan friars in Rome, Italy in response to the persecution and needs of the Church of his day.

2. Spiritual: The MI is spiritual in that it transforms the individual into another Mary, who is the perfect disciple of Christ. In the New Testament, Mary is the Woman of Faith who was first to be graced and the first to respond to that grace. By imitating her and uniting ourselves with her, we become more perfect disciples and mothers of Christ and thus are more intimately united with Him as she was.

3. Theological: Consecration is founded on the solid theological foundation of deepening one's ultimate baptismal consecration as taught by the Fathers of the early Church, the Doctors of the Middle Ages and the Marian scholars and saints of the present day.

4. Ecclesial: The MI was declared by the Church to be universal, not particular, in its mission and has canonical approval by the Vatican of its statutes as an international public association of the faithful.

5. Apostolic: The MI was founded as a movement to bring all people to Christ through the Virgin Mary and thus is missionary at heart, as was the Virgin

Mary who was the first missionary to bring Christ to another at her visitation to Elizabeth.

Consecration Began at the Foot of the Cross

Marian Consecration did not begin with St. Louis de Montfort or St. Maximilian Kolbe. It began at the foot of the Cross where Christ, Himself, entrusted John the beloved disciple and us to Mary. In this act of consecration/entrustment we find both individual and ecclesial consecration, for John's presence at the foot of the Cross is not only as an individual, but he stands there as the representative of the Church that is being redeemed.

Sub Tuum Praesidium: (300)

This is the oldest known prayer to Mary. It dates back to 300 AD when it was found in writing on papyrus. The fact that it was found in writing around 300 AD is evidence that it was probably prayed orally even before that. It is quite possible that the prayer reflects a tradition that traces back to the apostolic period. It is a filial prayer of Christians who know Mary's motherly mercy and do not hesitate to seek her motherly protection. It shows that prayer was being addressed to Mary as Theotokos or "Mother of God" long before the Council of Ephesus vindicated the use of that title in 431 AD. St. Maximilian was known to have prayed this prayer daily.

We turn to you for protection,
Holy Mother of God.

Listen to our prayers and help us in our needs.
Save us from every danger,
Glorious and blessed Virgin.

St. John Damascene (675-749)

St. John Damascene was a Greek theologian and doctor of the Church who taught that Mary was the Divine Mother of God who was free from all stain of sin and assumed into heaven. He constantly expressed his devotion to the Mother of God.

What is sweeter than the Mother of God? She holds my mind captive; she has seized my tongue; on her, I meditate day and night. Since she is the Mother of the Word, she has words abundant.

If truly, as the sacred Word has taught us, the honor paid to our fellow servants testifies to our good will towards our common Master, how could we neglect honoring you who have brought forth your Master? . . .In this way we can better show our attachment to our Master.

Today, we too do linger in your presence, O Sovereign! I say again: Sovereign, Virgin Mother of God, and let us bind our souls, as to a steadfast and immovable anchor: to the hope that you are for us. Let us consecrate to you our spirit and soul, our body, our whole person. We wish to honor you, as far as we are able, with psalms, hymns and spiritual songs.

Turn your gaze on us, Noble Lady, Mother of the good Master, rule over and direct at your discretion all that concerns us; restrain the impulses of our shameful passions; guide us to the tranquil harbor of the divine will; make us worthy of future blessedness, of the beatific vision in the presence of the Word of God who was made flesh in you.

Fulbert of Chartres (960-1028)

St. Fulbert of Chartres was born in Italy near Rome, and studied at Reims and Chartres and later became bishop of Chartres. In his writings concerning the Virgin Mary he speaks of how one's Baptism is supported and deepened by consecrating oneself to the Virgin Mary.

Remember, O Lady, that in Baptism I was consecrated to the Lord and professed the Christian name with my lips. Unfortunately I have not observed what I have promised. Nevertheless I have been handed over to you and committed to your care by the Lord, the living and true God. Watch over the one who has been handed over to you; keep safe the one who has been committed to your protection.

St. Louis de Montfort (d. 1716)

He is perhaps the first great theologian of consecration as is understood in the present day. He always underlined the fact that any consecration was necessarily made to "God alone" and only through or by means of Mary. Jesus is the goal of the act of consecration which De Montfort proposes, while Mary is its intermediary.

While he readily and very frequently speaks of "consecrating oneself to Mary," this must always be understood as a shorthand form of "consecrating oneself to Jesus through the hands of Mary."

"O admirable Mother, present me to your dear Son as His slave now and for always, so that He who redeemed me through you, will now receive me through you."

He spoke of true devotion to Mary as a renewal of one's baptismal promises, "through the hands of Mary." Consecration therefore could be called a perfect renewal of the vows and promises of Baptism. Before Baptism every person is a slave of the devil and after Baptism is set free to become a slave of the Lord in which one finds true freedom.

In De Montfort is seen the culmination of the concept of Marian "servitude" or "slavery." At first the notion of slavery is repulsive, yet Jesus Himself speaks of us as being slaves or servants in many of His parables and uses this imagery in many of His teachings. Jesus Himself is the Suffering Servant; the One who came not to be served but to serve. In this sense, slavery to Christ expresses the fullness of freedom that one finds in serving Christ.

According to St. Louis,

Our whole perfection consists in being conformed, united and consecrated to Jesus Christ; this consists in giving oneself entirely to the Blessed Virgin, in order to belong entirely to Jesus Christ through her.

Thus the soul becomes Mary's slave of love whereby we put ourselves totally in the hands and the service of Mary for the love of God. The entrustment must be lived by "performing all one's actions through Mary, with Mary, in Mary and for Mary, so as to perform them more perfectly through Jesus Christ, with Jesus Christ, in Jesus and for Jesus."

Maximilian Kolbe OFM CONV. (1894-1941)

The Ideal of the MI

The principal characteristic of Kolbe's consecration is its unlimitedness.

The outward sign of consecration is the Miraculous Medal. Though it is not essential, it is the integral sign and condition for our consecration.

The Founder of the Militia of the Immaculata wrote,

The ideal of every member of the M.I. is to be the servant and child of the Immaculate, and this out of love, as a slave, as Her property and possession, irrevocably and forever. It is our ideal to become Her own.

Kolbe strove for an identification with the Immaculata. He strove to imitate her in her openness to the Holy Spirit, her continuous "Yes" to God, and her perfect discipleship of Christ. By consecrating himself to the Immaculata, he believed that this was how he could give the greatest glory to God, through her who was God's most perfect creation and which none better could or ever would exist as taught by the Franciscan theologian, St. Bonaventure.

Consecration and the Immaculate Conception

Kolbe's consecration to Mary is centered around her Immaculate Conception, her relationship with Jesus as Mother, and the Holy Spirit as Spouse. Because she is without sin, the will of the Immaculate is strictly and perfectly united to the Will of the Holy Spirit. That is why in consecrating ourselves to the Immaculate One and doing her will, we are also giving ourselves to Jesus to do His Will.

Her will does not differ from the Will of God. Calling upon her will without reserve, you manifest a love for the Will of God, for her will is so perfect that in nothing does it differ from God's.

As the Immaculate Conception, therefore, it is impossible for Mary to be a barrier or wall between God and us for she is perfectly and totally united to God and incapable of doing anything apart from the Will of God. Therefore anyone who is united with Mary is united with God.

We imitate good, virtuous, holy people, but none of these is without imperfection; only she, Immaculate from the first moment of her existence, knows no imperfection, not the slightest fall. It is for us to imitate her, to come near to Her, to become like her, to become her own.

It is because of sin that our will differs from the Will of God. When we sin, we will something other than what God wills. Because Mary was conceived without sin, at no time has she ever willed anything other than what God wills. Therefore, Mary's will and the Will of God are one and the same as ours will be in the Kingdom of Heaven.

The Mediation of the Immaculata

Kolbe does not view consecration as a passage from Mary to Christ, but with Mary to Christ. She is not only one to whom we pray, but also one who leads the way and who journeys with us to the Kingdom of Heaven.

The object of all devotion is God. Devotion to Mary is a direct means to this end. We pass with Mary to the Other.

The Son of God became flesh and dwelt among us through the Virgin Mary. Her role in the history of salvation is not merely biological but also spiritual. Her spiritual role continues until the end of time as she continues to be the instrument through whom Christ comes to us and we to Him. Mary's mediation did not end in the biological realm of motherhood (giving birth) but continues in the spiritual realm of giving birth to Christ in our hearts in union with the Holy Spirit.

Mary is the one through whose intercession men reach Jesus and the one through whom Jesus reaches men.

Kolbe's Mariology is centered around a series of mediations of Jesus and the Holy Spirit. While some view mediations other than that of Jesus' mediation as walls that separate us or get in the way between us and Christ, Kolbe viewed them as doors and windows, especially the mediation of Mary, through which the Son of God shines in our lives and enters into our hearts and souls.

The union between the Immaculate and the Holy Spirit is so inexpressible, yet so perfect that the Holy Spirit acts only by the Immaculata His Spouse.

This action could not take place if there was no perfect union between the Holy Spirit and Mary. In an imperfect way, man and woman become one flesh in the Sacrament of Marriage. As the Spouse of the Holy Spirit who is without sin, Mary is perfectly united in will and spirit with the Holy Spirit.

Maximilian teaches that the same Mother who bore Christ, now through the power of her Spouse, the Holy Spirit, assists us in conceiving Christ and thus continues her ministry of Divine Motherhood and bearing Christ for the world.

Only at the last judgment, only in heaven will we discover with what loving attention our heavenly Mother watched over each one of us without ceasing, over every soul individually, because all are her children. She strives to shape them after the model of Jesus, her first-born Son.

Kolbe and De Montfort

Some people try to make great distinctions between St. Louis de Montfort and St. Maximilian Kolbe. While there are some distinctions, the consecration is identical because they both consist of a total giving of oneself to Christ through the Virgin Mary. For this reason, one who is already consecrated according to the formula of St. Louis de Montfort is not re-consecrated when they join the MI. They merely enroll in the MI and continue to live their consecration as a member of the MI. Do not, therefore, make too much of the differences between Kolbe and De Montfort.

1. St. Louis de Montfort did not speak of Mary as conceived without sin because at the time he was living, even though the Immaculate Conception was a widely held teaching in the Catholic Church, it had not yet been declared a dogma. He prefers to use biblical language centered around covenant and makes reference to Baptism as the ultimate consecration from which all other consecrations flow. St. Maximilian Kolbe, however, based his consecration, theology and relationship with Mary on the Immaculate Conception.

2. St. Maximilian Kolbe did not like references to slavery, as found throughout the writings of St. Louis de Montfort in reference to consecration to Mary. He does, however, refer to one as becoming the possession and property of Mary. Is there much distinction

between being a slave and her possession and property? Not really! The intent of both is a total giving over of oneself entirely to Mary without any reserve whatsoever.

3. Kolbe wished to make consecration active and dynamic in order to respond to the attacks against the Church and the rise of secularism and atheism. The MI therefore is apostolically oriented and, as a movement actively seeks to bring others to Christ through evangelizing consecration to the Immaculata. Thus, belonging to the MI means to belong to a worldwide movement whereby the members, by living their consecration and evangelizing it, bring the world to Christ through Mary.

In discussing consecration to the Blessed Virgin Mary one must begin with the Scriptures, and build on the Fathers of the Church; from Thomas Aquinas, Bonaventure, and Duns Scotus of the Middle Ages, to St. Louis de Montfort with Kolbe as the pinnacle of Marian thought and devotion. This clearly shows an unbroken historical and theological thread of consecration in the Church.

Becoming Another Mary

Consecration is more than a devotion. It is a life-changing event. St. Maximilian knew this personally as did all those before him who entrusted themselves to Mary and entered into a deep and personal relationship with her. St. Maximilian strove to express this inexpressible experience as best as he could by stating that when one is consecrated it is as if one is being transubstantiated into another Mary!

Just as the bread and wine at Mass are transubstantiated into the Body and Blood of Christ, so through consecration it is as if one is transubstantiated into another Mary. Please note that he says it is "as if" one is transubstantiated into another Mary. Here he is grasping for words that do not exist as to how intimate and transforming the act of consecration to Mary is. By consecrating ourselves to Mary, Mary lives in us and we in Mary. We become transformed into another Mary. What does it mean to become another Mary?

> *If we become like Mary, then we are "blessed and highly favored."*
> *We are overshadowed by the Holy Spirit.*
> *We become the Ark, the dwelling place of God.*
> *We give birth to Christ again in the world.*
> *We become the spouse of the Holy Spirit.*
> *We become the perfect disciple of Christ.*
> *We become an intercessor as she did at Cana.*
> *We share in the sufferings of Christ and stand at the foot of his Cross.*
> *Our hearts are pierced by a sword.*
> *We are at enmity with the devil.*

Is this not what we all long to become? Thus in becoming like Mary, we are totally and perfectly united in and with Christ and thus are transformed into Christ.

Entrustment

Entrustment is a word used often by Pope John Paul II in reference to Mary, but was used even before him. There is a debate as to whether or not entrustment is the same as consecration. Pope John Paul has used entrustment consistently in interpreting the text of John. 19:25-27. Entrusting oneself totally to Mary, according to the Holy Father means "accepting Mary into our lives."

> *As Mary gave birth to Christ, the Head of the Mystical Body, she also had to have given birth to all the members of that one Body. Entrusting himself to Mary in a filial manner, the Christian, like the Apostle John, welcomes the Mother of Christ into his own home.*
> —Pope John Paul II

Entrustment in the English language is less theological and easier to understand and needs little explanation. People often entrust their possessions and even their children and loved ones to another to care for them. Entrustment to the Immaculata can be thought of and explained in much the same way as giving ourselves to her for her love and protection.

On the other hand, the word consecration has been the favored word for almost two centuries, and bespeaks sacredness, a setting apart and a theological depth that entrustment does not.

Both are appropriate terms and at times can be used interchangeably and at other times distinctly.

Consecration

St. Louis de Montfort argues in favor of Marian consecration because it is the most direct way to Jesus. St. Maximilian Kolbe believes that going through Mary maximizes the value of all our acts. Pope John Paul II continues the teachings of these two saints by insisting that this is expressly the Will of Christ.

Traditional definitions of consecration to Mary consist in "offering oneself entirely to Mary, in order, through her, to belong totally to Jesus."

This is in imitation of the Son of God, who offered Himself entirely to Mary in order, through her, to belong totally to us.

Consecration properly called is nothing else but divinization: the transformation of human life into divine life, which is first offered by God and accepted by our free will.

Renewing One's Consecration Daily

Kolbe stated that we can consecrate ourselves to the Immaculate One in various ways, and express it in differently constructed forms and words; in fact, a simple act of will would suffice, for that really is the essence of such a consecration. Each day one should renew one's consecration to the Immaculata either by a written formula such as the prayer of consecration composed by St. Maximilian, or by the giving of one's heart and soul, life and eternity to the Immaculata in one's own words and desires.

There does exist, however a certain formula which would embody the spirit of the M.I.:

O Immaculata, Queen of heaven and Earth,
Refuge of sinners, and our most loving Mother,
God has willed to entrust the entire order of mercy to you.
I (name), *a repentant sinner,*
cast myself at your feet,
humbly imploring you to take me with all that I am and have,
wholly to yourself as your possession and property.
Please make of me,
of all my powers of soul and body,
of my whole life, death and eternity,
whatever most pleases you.
If it pleases you,
use all that I am and have without reserve,
wholly to accomplish what was said of you:
"She will crush your head,"
and "You alone have destroyed all heresies in the whole world."
Let me be a fit instrument in your immaculate and merciful hands,
for introducing and increasing your glory to the maximum,
in all the many strayed and indifferent souls,
and thus help extend as far as possible,
the blessed Kingdom of the most Sacred Heart of Jesus.
For wherever you enter,
you obtain the grace of conversion and growth in holiness,
since it is through your hands that all graces come to us,
from the most Sacred heart of Jesus.

V. Allow me to praise you, O Sacred Virgin
R. Give me strength against your enemies.

Introduction

We already have a relationship with Mary from the moment of our Baptism into the Church. She alone is the "perfected" Church, without spot or blemish, as St. Paul puts it, because she has already achieved what we only hope to become at the end of time. Thus, in Christ, she is the first member of the Church with whom we are joined, for she has become the model of the Church and, by association with the Redeemer, also its chief intercessor. Total consecration simply makes our relationship with Mary explicit and more effective.

St. Maximilian Kolbe himself realized that not everyone understands or is spiritually ready to make a total consecration. This does not imply that such a person is spiritually immature. Rather, each of us has personal insights and patterns of growth.

Sometimes a negative encounter with an imprudent client of Mary may have made us wary, unfortunately, of Marian devotion. Nevertheless, there is scarcely any Catholic who fails to pay tribute to her at least occasionally. Total consecration, however, is undoubtedly the most perfect way of establishing a personal bond with Mary and recognizing the spiritual process that occurs in each Christian soul, whether we are aware of it or not.

Besides the possibility of making an individual commitment to this Marian movement, a group, a club, a family, a religious province, a parish can make the total consecration. In such cases, individuals within a group may not consider themselves ready, but they can authentically commit themselves as a part of the group in the sense of consecrating at least what relates to the parish or province or family as such: its objectives and goals, relationships and communication, common prayers and aspirations.

Of course, the effectiveness of a corporate consecration will depend on how each person practices it with perseverance. Individual self-giving is always at the level of one's own spiritual growth.

Total consecration is not a light matter, not just another "devotion," but a complete spirituality based on one's sense of powerlessness as one of the anawim, the "little ones" of the Bible. This should emerge in the readings and reflections of this book; the latter are motivational in nature, not treatises and systematic theology. Nor are they a defense of Mary's privileges, designed to "convert" the reader. Rather, we review age-old doctrines, not to rediscover them—because they have not been lost—but to see them with a new vision and motive.

Once we see total consecration as a practical consequence of our Baptism, we realize it commits us to the evangelization of the world. We do not become fanatics or unrealistic, but we realize how many Catholics are merely nominal in the practice of their faith. They too have not really heard the Good News of Jesus in a way that has changed their lives. If the lives of saints are to be followed and not merely admired, then we have to trust their spiritual gifts—and I know of none who were not the clients of Mary. Yet the saints are our models of ministry and evangelization.

There is some danger in thinking that Marian spirituality is an option. It is simply an historical fact that the Incarnation took place in the Virgin's womb, that Jesus on the Cross gave His Mother to us, that she has achieved the glorious state we merely hope for. One meets Mary at every point of the way to Jesus as the model of our own relationship. Perhaps the decline in Marian spirituality in some lives is linked to their lack of faith in the mysteries of Jesus Himself!

Let us not be slow in sharing our Marian vision with others in our group or family or parish. Sometimes we fail to open our spiritual treasures to those we ought to love most! There is a natural reticence in speaking about one's personal spiritual life. But if we believe, why should we be fearful of giving witness to God's wonderful works through Mary in our lives? We call her the Mother of Hope, extending instruction in the First Letter of Peter to this context: "Should anyone ask you the reason for this hope of yours, be ever ready to reply" (3:15).

I have several suggestions for using this nine-day preparation, whether individually or as a group. The nine days need not be consecutive, although that is preferable. Perhaps the annual retreat is an appropriate time to prepare for total consecration.

If you cannot read and pray in a church or chapel conveniently, make a "sacred time and place" for yourself: a room without distraction, but with a cross and an image of Our Lady. For some, a secluded garden or other outdoor setting is a help to prayer. Most essential is the decision not to rush through the readings and prayers just to complete the texts. You cannot worry about being "productive" and covering a certain amount of material and expect to receive the visitation of God. Prayer is partly talking and partly listening.

During the period of preparation for total consecration you might think of making a general confession of your life. You should try to attend Mass and receive Holy Communion particularly on days of preparation. [The procedure for consecration, joining the MI and receiving the plenary indulgence is described on pages 87 and 88—Ed.]

When you have a convenient time, read the supplemental material in this book: the chronology of St. Maximilian, the catechism about the Militia of the Immaculata, the ritual of total consecration (which may be modified as you please). It goes without saying that praying at least part of the Rosary each day is common to Marian spirituality.

—Fr. Anselm Romb, OFM CONV.

Total Consecration
A Nine-day Preparation

DAY ONE
Mary, Spouse of the Holy Spirit, Nurtures Christ and the Church

St. Augustine's Prayer to the Holy Spirit

Breathe in me O Holy Spirit that my thoughts may all be holy;
Act in me O Holy Spirit that my works, too, may be holy;
Draw my heart O Holy Spirit that I love but what is holy;
Strengthen me O Holy Spirit to defend all that is holy;
Guard me then O Holy Spirit that I always may be holy.

Reading: Luke 1:26-38

In the sixth month, the angel Gabriel was sent from God to a town of Galilee called Nazareth, to a virgin betrothed to a man named Joseph, of the house of David, and the virgin's name was Mary. And coming to her, he said, "Hail, full of grace! The Lord is with you." But she was greatly troubled at what was said and pondered what sort of greeting this might be. Then the angel said to her, "Do not be afraid, Mary, for you have found favor with God. Behold, you will conceive in your womb and bear a son, and you shall name him Jesus. He will be great and will be called Son of the Most High, and the Lord God will give him the throne of David his father, and he will rule over the house of Jacob forever, and of his kingdom there will be no end."

But Mary said to the angel, "How can this be, since I have no relations with a man?" And the angel said to her in reply, "The Holy Spirit will come upon you, and the power of the Most High will overshadow you. Therefore the child to be born will be called holy, the Son of God. And behold, Elizabeth, your relative, has also conceived a son in her old age, and this is the sixth month for her who was called barren; for nothing is impossible for God." Mary said, "Behold, I am the handmaid of the Lord. May it be done to me according to your word." Then the angel departed from her.

Commentary

The Incarnation takes place in Mary's womb; the greatest event of history occurs at the Annunciation. The angel greets Mary with superlatives and indicates her primary role as Mother of the Messiah! At this moment the Holy Spirit verifies Mary as His "spouse" and that no human father will be the agent of conception.

Mary's generous response sets the tone of her whole life

with Jesus. She is the first and best Christian, our example of giving an unqualified "yes" without knowing the future.

Reflection

St. Maximilian, a Conventual Franciscan, was influenced by his Order's having been the defender of the doctrine of the Immaculate Conception for six centuries before the definition of the dogma in 1854, and before the words of Mary at Lourdes, "I am the Immaculate Conception." This Conception took place, after the normal human encounter of her parents, in the womb of Mary's mother. God, of course, creates each human soul individually; He gifted Mary with utter freedom from sin because of her future motherhood.

In the relationships within the Trinity the only begotten Son is generated by the Father. As we use our human experience to understand what "Son" means, so He leads us to understand the Spirit as the "Uncreated Immaculate Conception." Thus the Holy Spirit, as it were, gives His own name to Mary: the Immaculate Conception, and chooses her for His bride.

By Christ's direct command from the Cross, "Behold your Mother," we are to be formed by the Holy Spirit in Mary's womb, not physically, of course, but by the process of spiritual formation. Our total consecration acknowledges this process. Whereas such a consecration is not necessary to salvation, it is an immense help. Our awareness of a commitment makes us conscious of our responsibility to evangelize the world and imitate Mary.

As Scripture has it, Jesus remains the Mediator with God, but we go to Jesus and then to God *with* Mary, and *with* the whole Church. Thus Mary continues her nurturing motherhood in every member of the Church and gives birth to the likeness of Jesus in all of us by the power of her Spouse, the Holy Spirit, the Uncreated Immaculate Conception.

The Words of St. Maximilian
(Journal reflection: "Our Purpose," August 1940)

The aim of creation, the end of man himself, is the love of God, Creator and Father, an ever greater love, the divinization of man, his return to God from whom he came, union with God, a fruitful love. So that love for the Father might become even more perfect, infinitely more perfect, the love of the Son Jesus, made itself manifest. But so that love for the Son might burn more intensely and thus enkindle a still more ardent love for the Father, there has come to help us the united love of the Holy Spirit and of the Immaculata, the mother full of mercy, the Mediatrix of all graces, an earthly creature like ourselves, who strongly attracts hearts to herself and to her motherly heart.

The love of the Father, the Son and the Holy Spirit flames eternally; the love of the Father, Jesus and the Immaculata knows no imperfection. Only man (not always and not in all things) responds imperfectly to this love with his own love. To arouse that love for the Immaculata, therefore, by enkindling it in one's own heart, to communicate this fire to those who live close to us, to set on fire with this love all souls and each one in particular—those who live now and those who will live in the future, to make this flame burst forth ever more intensely and without restrictions in ourselves and all over the earth: such is our purpose. Everything else is just a means.

An effect resembles the cause that produced it. Consequently every creature shows in itself some resemblance to God, the more perfect the creature is the more evident is this resemblance.

Even if we could establish thousands and thousands of degrees, each more perfect, each more spiritually pure than the last, there would still remain an infinite distance between even the most elevated of these degrees and the Source of Love itself. God bends down to his own creature and joins himself to it with a love that annihilates that whole infinite space; he counts his creature as part of his family, makes it one of his own offspring.

The soul is regenerated in the sacred waters of Baptism and thus becomes God's child. Water, which purifies everything over which it runs, is a symbol of her who purifies every soul that draws near to her. It is a symbol of the Immaculata, of her who is without stain. Upon one who is washed in this water the grace of the Holy Spirit descends. The Holy Spirit, the divine Spouse of the Immaculata, acts only in her and through her; he communicates supernatural life, the life of grace, the divine life, the sharing in divine love, in divinity. The child of God, as a member of the divine family, has God the Father for father and the Mother of God for mother. Then one has the Son of God for brother and becomes God's heir and is joined to the Persons of this divine family through love. Nor is that all. The Son of God selects spouses from among souls; he unites himself with them in a conjugal love, and through him they become the mothers of many, many other souls.

Sub Tuum Praesidium Prayer

We fly to thy patronage, O holy Mother of God; despise not our petitions in our necessities, but deliver us always from all dangers, O glorious and blessed Virgin. Amen.

Miraculous Medal Prayer

O Mary, conceived without sin, pray for us who have recourse to you, and for all who do not have recourse to you, especially the enemies of the Church and all those recommended to you.

DAY TWO
Mary's Humble Dependence on God
Leads to Her Glorification

St. Augustine's Prayer to the Holy Spirit

Breathe in me O Holy Spirit that my thoughts may all be holy;
Act in me O Holy Spirit that my works, too, may be holy;
Draw my heart O Holy Spirit that I love but what is holy;
Strengthen me O Holy Spirit to defend all that is holy;
Guard me then O Holy Spirit that I always may be holy.

Reading: Luke 1:39-56

During those days Mary set out and traveled to the hill country in haste to a town of Judah, where she entered the house of Zechariah and greeted Elizabeth. When Elizabeth heard Mary's greeting, the infant leaped in her womb, and Elizabeth, filled with the Holy Spirit, cried out in a loud voice and said, "Most blessed are you among women, and blessed is the fruit of your womb. And how does this happen to me, that the mother of my Lord should come to me? For at the moment the sound of your greeting reached my ears, the infant in my womb leaped for joy. Blessed are you who believed that what was spoken to you by the Lord would be fulfilled." And Mary said:

*My soul proclaims the greatness of the Lord;
my spirit rejoices in God my savior.*

For he has looked upon his handmaid's lowliness; behold, from now on will all ages call me blessed.

The Mighty One has done great things for me, and holy is his name.

His mercy is from age to age to those who fear him.

He has shown might with his arm, dispersed the arrogant of mind and heart.

He has thrown down the rulers from their thrones but lifted up the lowly.

The hungry he has filled with good things; the rich he has sent away empty.

He has helped Israel his servant, remembering his mercy, according to his promise to our fathers, to Abraham and to his descendants forever.

Mary remained with her about three months and then returned to her home.

Commentary

Mary sets out on her first mission of evangelization—to her own family. Her Spouse, the Holy Spirit, leads Elizabeth, as the text reads, to proclaim Mary "blessed" and the unborn Baptist to stir in her womb at Jesus' presence. Mary, deeply rooted in the Scriptures of Israel, joins her personal praise of God to the Jewish Testament phrases. She identifies herself as one of the biblical anawim, God's "little ones," who humbly depend on God to defend and provide for them. Mary is the exemplar of all believers who trust God absolutely on their spiritual journey.

Reflection

Without any arrogance, but with a divinely inspired revelation, Mary predicts that all generations to come will call her "blessed," just as her cousin did. Her glory was not of her own making, but God's gift. So again and again Mary's role is emphasized in theology, as well as Catholic consciousness. Her shrines at Czestochowa, Guadalupe, Lourdes, Fatima, and elsewhere testify to our human need to show love to our Mother. A believer is spiritually impoverished who allows a day to pass without some expression of fidelity to her prediction.

It is a mistake to think that the purpose of doctrinal statements and the building of shrines is simply to glorify her, however; she who has already received the maximum glorification from God in heaven needs no glory from us! It is rather we who need to venerate her as model and celebrate her mysteries as corollaries of the mysteries of Jesus Christ. However the sacred arts and sciences exhaust themselves in Mary's praise and name her "blessed," the reason is always the same: she escaped our solidarity in guilt. She is the Immaculate Conception, the Virgin Mother!

The Words of St. Maximilian
(Magazine article: "The Secret of Strength and Power," September 1925)

Sometimes one hears people complain: "I would like to

correct myself; I would like to be better, but I just can't!" In history we read about great leaders and conquerors who were not capable of dominating their own evil inclinations. One such, for instance, was the celebrated Alexander the Great, who died a premature death because of his licentious living. When we look about us, we observe the disappearance of all morality, which is really frightening, especially among the young. Indeed, truly diabolical associations are being formed which include crime and debauchery in their program.

How can we counteract this? In such circumstances it might seem to be a sign of humility to recognize one's own powerlessness, just as when people say: "I can't correct myself!" But in reality there is a secret sort of pride hidden there. All this shows is that they count on their own strength exclusively and think that they can do this or that, relying solely on their powers.

This is not true; it is a lie, because with our own strength alone, all by ourselves, without divine help, we are not capable of doing anything, absolutely anything (cf. Jn 15:5). What then should we do? Place ourselves totally, with unlimited trust, in the hands of divine mercy, of which Our Lady is by God's decree the personification. We must not trust in ourselves at all. We should fear ourselves, yet entrust ourselves to her without restriction and turn to her like a child to its mother whenever we feel ourselves incited to evil. Then we shall absolutely not fail. The saints affirm that whoever turns to her in trust during all his life will certainly be saved.

(Magazine article: "More Thinking!", November 1925)

Of course a heart corrupted by sin is fearful of eternity and hence avoids thinking about it. What can one do, then? Refusing to think about reality does not make it go away, so we have to think about it.

Well, now, we have a mother in heaven, the personification of divine mercy, the Immaculata. So then, if the thought of your past life and former sins torments you, if you do not have the courage to look at what is awaiting you beyond the grave, consecrate yourself totally and unreservedly to her. Entrust to her the whole problem of your salvation, your life, death and eternity. Confess your sins sincerely and trust fully in her. Then you will know what peace and happiness really are, a foretaste of paradise. And you will begin to yearn for it.

If you have never experienced all this, try it — see whether it is true or not — and you will find out.

Sub Tuum Praesidium Prayer

We fly to thy patronage, O holy Mother of God; despise not our petitions in our necessities, but deliver us always from all dangers, O glorious and blessed Virgin. Amen.

Miraculous Medal Prayer

O Mary, conceived without sin, pray for us who have recourse to you, and for all who do not have recourse to you, especially the enemies of the Church and all those recommended to you.

DAY THREE
Mary, the Virgin Mother, and Her Divine Son Fulfill the Longing of the Ages

St. Augustine's Prayer to the Holy Spirit

Breathe in me O Holy Spirit that my thoughts may all be holy;
Act in me O Holy Spirit that my works, too, may be holy;
Draw my heart O Holy Spirit that I love but what is holy;
Strengthen me O Holy Spirit to defend all that is holy;
Guard me then O Holy Spirit that I always may be holy.

Reading: Matthew 1:18-25

Now this is how the birth of Jesus Christ came about. When his mother Mary was betrothed to Joseph, but before they lived together, she was found with child through the Holy Spirit. Joseph her husband, since he was a righteous man, yet unwilling to expose her to shame, decided to divorce her quietly. Such was his intention when, behold, the angel of the Lord appeared to him in a dream and said, "Joseph, son of David, do not be afraid to take Mary your wife into your home. For it is through the Holy Spirit that this child has been conceived in her. She will bear a son and you are to name him Jesus, because he will save his people from their sins." All this took place to fulfill what the Lord had said through the prophet:

Behold, the virgin shall be with child and bear a son, and they shall name him "Emmanuel," which means "God is with us."

When Joseph awoke, he did as the angel of the Lord had commanded him and took his wife into his home. He had no relations with her until she bore a son, and he named him Jesus.

Commentary

The sacred writer is careful to point out the virginal state of Mary by relating Joseph's experience with the angel, as well as quoting the ancient prophecy of Isaiah (7:14) about the "virgin with child." As head of the family, Joseph was brought into the mystery of Jesus' birth. To Mary's heavenly Spouse, the Holy Spirit, is attributed her conception; to her earthly spouse is given the charge to name the child. Meanwhile Mary keeps silence, despite the anguish she must have suffered, and trusts God to explain her situation to her husband.

Reflection

Right after the Gospels were written, the first Fathers of the Church stressed Mary's virginity as a keystone of Christian theology. St. Ignatius of Antioch, for example, who was martyred in 116 AD, wrote in his Letter to the Ephesians that Mary's virginity, along with Jesus' birth and death, were the three great mysteries crying out to be proclaimed—thus an essential part of the Good News of the Christ, because Mary's virginity is the convalidation of Jesus' being the Son of God.

How sad to hear of some theologians who down-play or even deny Mary's privileges, as if God were limited in his power to arrange His own Son's birth. And did not the Son have the freedom to make His mother whatever He chose? Did the Holy Spirit set a boundary to His love of His spouse? Those who wish to be totally consecrated to Mary should study her relationships to the Three Divine Persons, come to know her virtues by meditation, and understand her role in salvation as revealed in the Scriptures.

The Words of St. Maximilian

(Journal reflection: "The Immaculata is Yours—You are Hers," August 1940)

This is why the Immaculata is our mother:

1. This is the common conviction, the belief of the faithful.

2. Jesus gave her to us.

3. She is the mother of the Church's Head, that is, Jesus, hence the mother of his members.

4. She is mother of divine grace, the grace of the Holy Spirit; she is the Mediatrix of Graces, mother of the life of grace, of the spiritual life.

5. She is the mother of the Redeemer, hence also mother of the redeemed, Co-redemptrix.

6. She is the mother of the Creator, hence the Mother of all creatures as well (angels, men, and so forth).

So you, my child, must love her as your mother with all the generosity of your heart. She loved you enough to sacrifice God's Son for you. In the Annunciation she welcomed you with all graciousness as her child. She will make you like herself, will make you ever more immaculate, will nourish you with the milk of her grace. Just let yourself be guided by her; let yourself be ever more willingly shaped by her. Watch over the purity of your conscience; purify it in her love. Do not get discouraged, even if you sin seriously, repeatedly. An act of perfect love will purify you again. You belong to her as her property. Let her do with you what she wishes. Do not let her feel herself bound by any restrictions flowing from the obligations a mother has towards her own child.

Be hers—her property. Let her make free use of you and dispose of you without any limits for whatever purpose she wishes. Let her be your owner, your Lady and absolute Queen. A servant sells his labor. You, on the contrary, offer yours as a gift: your fatigue, your suffering, all that is yours. Beg her not to pay attention to your free will, but to act towards you always as she desires in full liberty.

Be her child, her servant, her slave of love in every way and under whatever formulation yet devised or which can be devised now or in the future. In a word, be all hers. Be hers to the point of being her soldier, so that others may become ever more perfectly hers, like you yourself and even more than you; so that all those who live and will live all over the world may work together with her in her struggle against the infernal serpent. Belong to the Immaculata so that your conscience, becoming ever purer, may be purified still more; become immaculate, as she is for Jesus, so you, too, may become a mother and conqueror of hearts for her.

Sub Tuum Praesidium Prayer

We fly to thy patronage, O holy Mother of God; despise not our petitions in our necessities, but deliver us always from all dangers, O glorious and blessed Virgin. Amen.

Miraculous Medal Prayer

O Mary, conceived without sin, pray for us who have recourse to you, and for all who do not have recourse to you, especially the enemies of the Church and all those recommended to you.

DAY FOUR
Mary Joins Herself to Jesus for Our Redemption

St. Augustine's Prayer to the Holy Spirit

Breathe in me O Holy Spirit that my thoughts may all be holy;
Act in me O Holy Spirit that my works, too, may be holy;
Draw my heart O Holy Spirit that I love but what is holy;
Strengthen me O Holy Spirit to defend all that is holy;
Guard me then O Holy Spirit that I always may be holy.

Reading: Luke 2:22-40

When the days were completed for their purification according to the law of Moses, they took him up to Jerusalem to present him to the Lord, just as it is written in the law of the Lord, "Every male that opens the womb shall be consecrated to the Lord," and to offer the sacrifice of "a pair of turtledoves or two young pigeons," in accordance with the dictate in the law of the Lord.

Now there was a man in Jerusalem whose name was Simeon. This man was righteous and devout, awaiting the consolation of Israel, and the Holy Spirit was upon him. It had been revealed to him by the Holy Spirit that he should not see death before he had seen the Messiah of the Lord. He came in the Spirit into the temple; and when the parents brought in the child Jesus to perform the custom of the law in regard to him, he took him into his arms and blessed God, saying:

> *Now, Master, you may let your servant go in peace, according to your word,*
> *for my eyes have seen your salvation, which you prepared in sight of all the peoples,*
> *a light for revelation to the Gentiles, and glory for your people Israel.*

The child's father and mother were amazed at what was said about him; and Simeon blessed them and said to Mary his mother, "Behold, this child is destined for the fall and rise of many in Israel, and to be a sign that will be contradicted (and you yourself a sword will pierce) so that the thoughts of many hearts may be revealed." There was also a prophetess, Anna, the daughter of Phanuel, of the tribe of Asher. She was advanced in years, having lived seven years with her husband after her marriage, and then as a widow until she was eighty-four. She never left the temple, but worshiped night and day with fasting and prayer. And coming forward at that very time, she gave thanks to God and spoke about the child to all who were awaiting the redemption of Jerusalem. When they had fulfilled all the prescriptions of the law of the Lord, they returned to Galilee, to their own town of Nazareth. The child grew and became strong, filled with wisdom; and the favor of God was upon him.

Commentary

Mary and Joseph faithfully adhere to the Jewish law and consecrate the Boy to the Lord. The Holy Spirit again activates the mystery of Jesus as Simeon holds Him and proclaims the presence of the light of the world and glory of Israel. He foretells that the Child will be opposed in order to reveal the thoughts of many hearts. Mary, he predicts, will be directly linked to the suffering of the Messiah; she will be pierced by a sword. By the prophecy of Simeon the Holy Spirit prepares His spouse to enter deeply into the redemptive process alongside her Son.

Reflection

John's Gospel often uses individuals as "types," that is, symbols of whole groups or even of all human beings. In the dialogue with "the Mother of Jesus" and "the disciple whom Jesus loved," John makes the disciple stand in for all the world and the Church. By Jesus giving Mary to John as his mother, she becomes the mother of the Church and the world.

As a daughter of Israel, Mary had the pain of seeing her homeland overrun by the Romans. As a child of God she suffered from seeing her nation's leaders too concerned about external observances. After Jesus left home she had the uncertainty of poverty and fear for her Son's life. Then after seeing her Son die shamefully and enjoying His resurrected presence for a mere forty days, she witnessed the martyrdom of the early believers, the Mystical Body of which she was the Mother. Yet she continued to press the work of evangelization, becoming the prime source of knowledge for the events of Jesus' life, keeping His memory alive, strengthening the disciples, even though she was impatient to be homeward bound to possess what she had so long pondered.

The Words of St. Maximilian
(Magazine article: "Purpose of the Militia of the Immaculata," December 1937)

Strictly speaking, the mission of the Militia of the Immaculata is the same as that of the Immaculata herself. As Co-redemptrix, in fact, she desires to extend to all humanity the fruits of the redemption effected by her Son and to do all she can to win back to Christ heretics, schismatics, Freemasons, Jews, etc. The sole desire of the Immaculata is to lift the level of our spiritual life until it reaches the height of sanctity. She does not expect to bring about these goals of apostolic activity directly, in person. Rather, she seeks to involve us in them. Consequently the essential condition that every member of the Militia of the Immaculata should effectively realize is self-offering to the Immaculata as her own.

We can consecrate ourselves to the Immaculata by making use of any formula, as long as we renounce our own wills and adhere to her orders, which are made known to us in the commandments of God and of the Church, in the duties of our state in life, and in internal inspirations. This activity of the Immaculata will be all the more effective the more that we for our part seek to deepen our spiritual formation. Consecration to the Immaculata, therefore, implies the necessity of working for the perfection of ourselves and of our inclinations. Only when we are perfectly obedient to the Immaculata shall we become worthy instruments in her apostolic hands. We shall be apostles by the example of our lives, apostles by offering others the help of our actions.

Sub Tuum Praesidium Prayer

We fly to thy patronage, O holy Mother of God; despise not our petitions in our necessities, but deliver us always from all dangers, O glorious and blessed Virgin. Amen.

Miraculous Medal Prayer

O Mary, conceived without sin, pray for us who have recourse to you, and for all who do not have recourse to you, especially the enemies of the Church and all those recommended to you.

DAY FIVE
Mary, Our Model of Spirituality is Formed by Jesus

St. Augustine's Prayer to the Holy Spirit

Breathe in me O Holy Spirit that my thoughts may all be holy;
Act in me O Holy Spirit that my works, too, may be holy;
Draw my heart O Holy Spirit that I love but what is holy;
Strengthen me O Holy Spirit to defend all that is holy;
Guard me then O Holy Spirit that I always may be holy.

Reading: Luke 2:41-52

Each year his parents went to Jerusalem for the feast of Passover, and when he was twelve years old, they went up according to festival custom. After they had completed its days, as they were returning, the boy Jesus remained behind in Jerusalem, but his parents did not know it. Thinking that he was in the caravan, they journeyed for a day and looked for him among their relatives and acquaintances, but not finding him, they returned to Jerusalem to look for him.

After three days they found him in the temple, sitting in the midst of the teachers, listening to them and asking them questions, and all who heard him were astounded at his understanding and his answers.

When his parents saw him, they were astonished, and his mother said to him, "Son, why have you done this to us? Your father and I have been looking for you with great anxiety."

And he said to them, "Why were you looking for me? Did you not know that I must be in my Father's house?" But they did not understand what he said to them.

He went down with them and came to Nazareth, and was obedient to them; and his mother kept all these things in her heart. And Jesus advanced in wisdom and age and favor before God and man.

Commentary

As devout Jews, the Holy Family makes the Passover pilgrimage to Jerusalem, but Mary and Joseph lose track of Jesus on the way home. Mary's heart sinks when she finds the Boy in dialogue with the religious teachers; she wonders whether this is the time He must leave home to begin His ministry—and she knows she must let Him go. She does not grasp His answer about His "Father's house." But she accepts the guidance of her Son and returns home, keeping the event in her memory and pondering it in her heart.

Reflection

Three times in the Infancy Narrative of Luke, Mary is said to reflect on the events in Jesus' life: the Nativity, the Presentation, the Finding in the Temple. Mary is presented to us as the model of the Church's prayer life, and of living by the instruction of Jesus. After the pattern of Mary the Church reflects on her Head and cherishes what Jesus said and did. After His being found in the Temple, Jesus is said to grow in wisdom and grace and age. It is obvious that Mary also grew spiritually throughout her life.

No doubt Mary taught her Son how to be a more effective person on the human level, how to relate with women in His ministry, how to express feelings of mercy and tenderness and compassion. Jesus in turn taught her as His chief disciple how to understand the Jewish Testament about His own life's work, so that she was fully prepared to surrender her mother's rights, "let go" of Him, and even enter the mystery of the passion at His side.

Thus God involved Mary in His design, His "secret plan" hidden for ages, but revealed in Christ in the fullness of time. We, too, are called to search out God's plan and Mary's share in that mystery of salvation. We do not choose her as mother or queen; God has already chosen her. We are simply the beneficiaries of the gift of Mary's presence in the Church and in individual souls. By our total consecration, what begins in our lives as obedience to God's inspiration ends with joy and peace that we have made such a commitment!

The Words of St. Maximilian
(Journal reflection: "The Immaculate is Yours—You are Hers," August 1940)

You are hers, so let yourself be guided by the Immaculata.

1. Feel sure that she permits whatever does not

depend on your will for your own good, even if it arises from another evil will. She is the one who wants this to happen to you.

2. Meet a difficulty: a) by not paying attention to it as long as it neither helps nor hinders you in achieving your aim of drawing closer to her, of loving her, Jesus, and the Father, b) by making use of this circumstance—going along with it—if it can help you, or c) by opposing it, if it is an impediment to you. She wants you to act in this way.

3. In what religious obedience prescribes, her will, that of her Son, and that of the Father is obvious. Hence it must be infinitely wise, prudent, powerful and good, even if by the light of your reason you are not able to realize this, since your mind is limited and fallible.

4. By putting her will into practice you show genuine, substantial love for her, for Jesus and for the Father. You become holy.

5. Whatever the Father wills, the Son and the Holy Spirit will likewise. Jesus and the Immaculata will it, too; their wills never contradict each other.

6. In those matters where neither necessity nor obedience decides, act as you wish, seeking to please her. "Love, and do what you will," as St. Augustine said.

7. Keep your conscience pure; be careful not to fall. But if you do fall, hasten to rise again.

8. She will keep you from falling if you place your trust in her, not relying at all on yourself—if you do on your part what you can, not to fall, with her help.

9. The reason for a fall is over-confidence in one's own strength. The truth is that by ourselves we are nothing and can do nothing. Without her, the Mediatrix of Grace, we cannot keep from falling.

10. If you do fall, offer yourself to her right away, with the whole sorry business of your fall, and beg for pardon. "Dearest 'Mom,' pardon me, and ask Jesus to pardon me, too." Try to perform your next action in such a way as to give the greatest possible joy to her and to Jesus. Be sure that this act of love will completely wipe out your fault. In your next confession accuse yourself of that fault—but she, Jesus and the Father will already have forgotten it.

11. Love with your whole being, your whole will, your whole heart. But if you feel yourself dry and cannot elicit feelings of love, do not be concerned; this does not belong to the essence of love. If your will desires only to accomplish her will, be at peace, for you truly love her, Jesus and the Father.

12. Do not forget that holiness consists not in extraor-

dinary actions, but in performing well your duties toward God, yourself and others.

13. No one, and not even the holiest state of life, can guarantee that you will sanctify your soul if you neglect the duties proper to that state. Try to discover in these duties the certain will of the Immaculata. By fulfilling this you will demonstrate your love for her and in and through her for Jesus and the Father. Indeed, prayer, penance, and other works, even though good in themselves, are of no value in her eyes if they hinder you in the proper carrying out of your duties. In these alone you find her will.

14. You can, without hesitation, use expressions like "I desire to fulfill the Immaculata's will," "May the Immaculata's will be done," "The Immaculata wanted it this way," because she wills what Jesus wills, as Jesus wills what his Father wills. Thus her will differs in no way from that of her Son and of the Father.

Indeed, the very act of yielding yourself unreservedly to her will not only shows that you love the will of God, but also proclaims the truth that her will is so perfect that it deviates in nothing from the will of God. Thus you will give glory to God the Father and the Son, both for creating a creature as perfect as she is and for having made her his own mother.

Sub Tuum Praesidium Prayer

We fly to thy patronage, O holy Mother of God; despise not our petitions in our necessities, but deliver us always from all dangers, O glorious and blessed Virgin. Amen.

Miraculous Medal Prayer

O Mary, conceived without sin, pray for us who have recourse to you, and for all who do not have recourse to you, especially the enemies of the Church and all those recommended to you.

DAY SIX
Mary Leads Us to Obey Christ, the Head of the Church

St. Augustine's Prayer to the Holy Spirit

Breathe in me O Holy Spirit that my thoughts may all be holy;
Act in me O Holy Spirit that my works, too, may be holy;
Draw my heart O Holy Spirit that I love but what is holy;
Strengthen me O Holy Spirit to defend all that is holy;
Guard me then O Holy Spirit that I always may be holy.

Reading: John 2:1-11

On the third day there was a wedding in Cana in Galilee, and the mother of Jesus was there. Jesus and his disciples were also invited to the wedding. When the wine ran short, the mother of Jesus said to him, "They have no wine." And Jesus said to her, "Woman, how does your concern affect me? My hour has not yet come." His mother said to the servers, "Do whatever he tells you." Now there were six stone water jars there for Jewish ceremonial washings, each holding twenty to thirty gallons. Jesus told them, "Fill the jars with water." So they filled them to the brim. Then he told them, "Draw some out now and take it to the headwaiter." So they took it. And when the headwaiter tasted the water that had become wine, without knowing where it came from (although the servers who had drawn the water knew), the headwaiter called the bridegroom and said to him, "Everyone serves good wine first, and then when people have drunk freely, an inferior one; but you have kept the good wine until now." Jesus did this as the beginning of his signs in Cana in Galilee and so revealed his glory, and his disciples began to believe in him.

Commentary

This text relates the first of Jesus' public signs, which led to His disciples' believing in Him. He appears to advance the time of his charismatic ministry at the insistence of His Mother. Her motive is so human, so down-to-earth: to save a groom embarrassment at a time when he was scarcely thinking of his guests! Jesus adds His special touch to the party; He provides not just any wine, but a choice vintage. Jesus and Mary always bring joy and harmony to all our mundane activities, if we but give them access to our lives.

Reflection

Generally St. John's Gospel mentions significant persons by name, but at Cana and Calvary, he simply uses the title, "Mother of Jesus." He alone records that Jesus addresses Mary as "woman," a title of respect in a formal situation. It was as if Jesus was formally denoting the place of Mary in the believing community for all time. In fact, He both opens and closes His public life with a dialogue with her: at Cana and Calvary. This surely indicates her importance at critical junctures of human life, because the Gospels have significance for all times and all persons, beyond the simple narration of Jesus' personal history.

At Cana Mary does not ask for anything in particular, but just tells her Son about the lack of wine at the party, knowing He will take care of the need. At Calvary she accepts John and all of us as her children, once more without asking anything.

Will she do less for us today who wish to call her "Mother"? Does Jesus refuse her anything when she makes known our needs? Her only command in the Scriptures is, "Do whatever He tells you." She leads us to obey Christ. She does not judge us, but simply receives us.

When Jesus told us to be perfect as our heavenly Father is perfect, He must have meant for us to love others unconditionally and forgive—because who but God can forgive sins? So Mary loves us unconditionally and forgives us when we forget her or turn away momentarily in our sins. But she is interested, as is God himself—for their wills are the same—in making us more worthy of grace now and more ready for God's judgment at death. Our ideal, then, as we consecrate ourselves totally, is to deepen that love relationship with her and carry the message of her power and mercy to everyone we know, first to our family and friends and co-workers, then to our parish and community and neighborhood, finally to all nations and all hearts. But our effectiveness will flow from consecrating our bodies and souls, all our powers and virtues, every relationship and human experience.

The Words of St. Maximilian
(Magazine article: "On the MI," December 1936)

The ideal of those who join [the Militia of the Immaculata] is to belong to the Immaculata, to be her servant, child, slave, property—in a word, to be hers under whatever title which love for her has ever thought of or will be ever capable of thinking to belong to her in all aspects during one's whole life, death, and eternity: to be hers without any restriction, irrevocably and forever hers; to become ever more totally hers, more perfectly hers, more like her, more one with her; to become in some fashion her very self; so that she may take possession of our souls more fully, may master them entirely, and in them and through them may think, speak, love God and others, and act. Such is the ideal: to become hers, to be "of the Immaculata."

Whoever becomes her possession in an increasingly perfect manner, in this fashion will exercise an ever greater influence in the milieu in which he is placed and will spur others on to know the Immaculata ever more perfectly, to love her ever more ardently, to draw ever closer to her, and to consecrate oneself to her to the point of becoming totally and without any limitation *her* very self. A soul of this kind, totally possessed by the Immaculata, will conquer an increasing number of souls for her, using every legitimate means, and will become not only her property, but her knight, a soldier of the Immaculata!

Sub Tuum Praesidium Prayer

We fly to thy patronage, O holy Mother of God; despise not our petitions in our necessities, but deliver us always from all dangers, O glorious and blessed Virgin. Amen.

Miraculous Medal Prayer

O Mary, conceived without sin, pray for us who have recourse to you, and for all who do not have recourse to you, especially the enemies of the Church and all those recommended to you.

DAY SEVEN
*Mary, the New Eve
and Mother of the Church*

St. Augustine's Prayer to the Holy Spirit

Breathe in me O Holy Spirit that my thoughts may all be holy;
Act in me O Holy Spirit that my works, too, may be holy;
Draw my heart O Holy Spirit that I love but what is holy;
Strengthen me O Holy Spirit to defend all that is holy;
Guard me then O Holy Spirit that I always may be holy.

Reading: Genesis 3:14-20

Then the Lord God said to the serpent:

Because you have done this, you shall be banned from all the animals and from all the wild creatures;
On your belly shall you crawl, and dirt shall you eat all the days of your life.
I will put enmity between you and the woman, and between your offspring and hers;
He will strike at your head, while you strike at his heel.

To the woman he said:

> *I will intensify the pangs of your childbearing; in pain shall you bring forth children. Yet your urge shall be for your husband, and he shall be your master.*

To the man he said:

> *Because you listened to your wife and ate from the tree of which I had forbidden you to eat,*
> *Cursed be the ground because of you! In toil shall you eat its yield all the days of your life.*
> *Thorns and thistles shall it bring forth to you, as you eat of the plants of the field.*
> *By the sweat of your face shall you get bread to eat,*
> *Until you return to the ground, from which you were taken;*
> *For you are dirt, and to dirt you shall return.*

The man called his wife Eve, because she became the mother of all the living.

Commentary

This text provides the first promise of the Savior to come, the only balm to the painful curse upon our race. The snake, symbol for Satan, will be crushed under the heel of Eve's offspring, who is eminently Jesus Christ, of course. The Church has also applied this passage to Mary, who is the enemy of the tempter. Since we are Mary's children by adoption and consecration, the warfare is carried on today by us, her "offspring."

Reflection

Humankind's capacity for good was not entirely destroyed by original sin, only impaired. God made several covenants with the chosen people and finally through Christ with the Church. The possibility of a sacred relationship with God flowered most perfectly when in the fullness of time Mary conceived the Savior. Her fullness of grace reversed the triple alienation of our first parents from God, one another, and nature itself. She has made it possible to restore paradise even on earth to those who establish harmony and reason in their own triple relationships.

Some Christians, hesitant in their commitment to Mary, point out that she appears in only a few passages of the Gospels, only once in the Epistles, and only mysteriously in Revelation. Yet it is not the number of passages, but their significance that counts. The Christian Testament is not a detailed biography of Jesus as such, but rather His Good News as proclaimed by the first believing community. That community recorded Mary's role at the significant times of Jesus' life, her modeling as the "ponderer" of sacred events, her consent to the Incarnation, her presence at the Cross and on Pentecost, her hearing the Word of God and keeping it, her symbolizing the perfect discipleship.

The totally consecrated person likewise ponders the Christian mysteries and joins his or her life to that of Jesus and Mary. Total consecration is also a "covenant" made by an act of the will. It does not lie in feeling, but in action. The fact that one does not repudiate this covenant, but tries to remember it as often as possible and live by its implications concretely suffices for its effectiveness. One can scarcely have a continuous awareness all day long of one's consecration. We do our duty and know we belong to her entirely.

The Words of St. Maximilian
(Magazine article: "The First Condition," May 1922)

The aim of the Militia of the Immaculata is so difficult to achieve, that if we relied only on natural energy, activity, and effort, we could with reason doubt about the possibility of achieving it. Daily experience, in fact, teaches us that the Church's enemies have more abundant natural means, and often, as Christ has told us, they are wiser in their own ways than the children of light. Further, to obtain the conversion and sanctification of souls, grace is needed, whereas corrupt nature tends by its own inclination towards sin. Consequently we can count solely on help from on high.

In this area the easiest and surest help is, by God's Will, the most holy Virgin Mary. To her the Church applies the words of the Holy Scripture: "She shall crush your head" (Gn 3:15), that is, of the infernal serpent. Of her the Church sings: "You have overcome all heresies in the whole world" (Office of the Blessed Virgin Mary).

Furthermore, history teaches that no conversion ever has taken place without a particularly evident presence of Mary's hand (all the saints have entertained a special devotion towards her), while Pope Leo XIII affirms in an encyclical on the Rosary: "It can be said that by a divine disposition nothing can be communicated to us from the infinite treasure of grace except through Mary. Thus just as no one can draw near to the Father save by means of the

Son, so too ordinarily no one can draw near to Christ except by means of his mother."

Can we, therefore, set about our task of fulfilling the purpose of the Militia of the Immaculata in any other way than by consecrating ourselves unreservedly, totally, and forever to the most Blessed Virgin Mary Immaculate, to be instruments in her hands so that she herself may act in us and through us? A consecration of this kind, therefore, constitutes the essence of the Militia of the Immaculata.

Sub Tuum Praesidium Prayer

We fly to thy patronage, O holy Mother of God; despise not our petitions in our necessities, but deliver us always from all dangers, O glorious and blessed Virgin. Amen.

Miraculous Medal Prayer

O Mary, conceived without sin, pray for us who have recourse to you, and for all who do not have recourse to you, especially the enemies of the Church and all those recommended to you.

DAY EIGHT
Mary, Model of Faith

St. Augustine's Prayer to the Holy Spirit

Breathe in me O Holy Spirit that my thoughts may all be holy;

Act in me O Holy Spirit that my works, too, may be holy;

Draw my heart O Holy Spirit that I love but what is holy;

Strengthen me O Holy Spirit to defend all that is holy;

Guard me then O Holy Spirit that I always may be holy.

Reading: Mark 3:31-35

His mother and his brothers arrived. Standing outside they sent word to him and called him. A crowd seated around him told him, "Your mother and your brothers (and your sisters) are outside asking for you." But he said to them in reply, "Who are my mother and (my) brothers?" And looking around at those seated in the circle he said, "Here are my mother and my brothers. (For) whoever does the Will of God is my brother and sister and mother."

Commentary

The family of Jesus interrupts His teaching. He remarks that even the closest physical kinship must cede to the spiritual kinship He is generating with his listeners, based on their fulfilling the Will of His heavenly Father. While not disparaging His own Mother, Jesus gently continues to form her with His spiritual direction. His words also reveal the true source of Mary's greatness, for she had already heard the word of God and kept it with such perfection that she had become the virgin Mother of the Incarnate Word, the biblical sign of the Church's perfect relationship with Christ.

Reflection

We cannot approach the mysteries of Mary without the illumination of her Spouse, the Holy Spirit, who scrutinizes all matters, even the deep things of God (1 Cor 2:10). If she seems remote, an untouchable figure on a pedestal, it may be because we have not striven to know her, talk with her in prayer, see how she combined an obscure humdrum life with great sanctity. It has been said that it is difficult, at times, for a person to relate positively with our heavenly Mother if that person has had a poor relationship with his or her human mother. Yet the point is that Jesus is the pattern of our other relationships—and He forever calls her "Mother."

Surely Jesus continues His filial respect and love for her even in heaven, and accepts her intercession for clients! We recall that Jesus said, "Who is my Mother? . . . whoever does the Will of my Father in heaven" (Mt 12:48). No doubt Mary was without equal in this obedience by her continual *fiat*. She was the greatest and most gifted person as Virgin and Mother, but she was the most perfect disciple and co-worker because she pondered God's Word and lived by its implications. The totally consecrated person will do no less.

The Words of St. Maximilian
("Who is She?" Sketches for a book, 1940)

Of herself, Mary is nothing, even as all other creatures are; but by God's gift she is the most perfect of creatures, the most perfect image of God's divine being in a purely human creature.

She comes, then, from the Father, through the Son and the Holy Spirit, as from her Creator who, out of nothing, calls into being creatures made in His own image, the image of the Holy Trinity. These creatures are limited; yet God likes to find in them the image of Himself which they bear. These beings, endowed with reason and free will, know and acknowledge that they come from God and receive everything from Him: what they are, what they can do, what they possess moment by moment. In return, they show Him their love, both on account of what they receive from Him, and because he, God, the infinite perfection, is worthy of infinite love.

The Immaculata never knew the slightest stain; in other words, her love was always full, without flaw. She loved God with all her being, and from the first instance of her existence her love united with God so perfectly that on the day of the Annunciation the Angel could say to her, "Full of grace! The Lord is with thee!" (cf. Lk 1: 28) She is, then, God's creature, God's image, God's child, and in all these respects she is all this in the most perfect manner possible among the ranks of mere creatures.

She is God's instrument. With full consciousness and total willingness she allows God to govern her; she consents to his will, desires only what he desires, and acts according to his will in the most perfect manner, without failing, without ever turning aside from his will. She makes perfect use of the powers and privileges God has given her, so as to fulfill always and in everything whatever God wants of her, purely for love of God, One and Three. This love of God reaches such a peak that it bears the divine fruits proper to God's own love. Her love for God brings her to such a level of union with him that she becomes the Mother of God. The Father confides to her his Son; the Son descends into her womb; and the Holy Spirit fashions out of her perfectly pure body the very Body of Jesus.

Sub Tuum Praesidium Prayer

We fly to thy patronage, O holy Mother of God; despise not our petitions in our necessities, but deliver us always from all dangers, O glorious and blessed Virgin. Amen.

Miraculous Medal Prayer

O Mary, conceived without sin, pray for us who have recourse to you, and for all who do not have recourse to you, especially the enemies of the Church and all those recommended to you.

DAY NINE
Jesus Entrusts His Disciples to Mary

St. Augustine's Prayer to the Holy Spirit

Breathe in me O Holy Spirit that my thoughts may all be holy;
Act in me O Holy Spirit that my works, too, may be holy;
Draw my heart O Holy Spirit that I love but what is holy;
Strengthen me O Holy Spirit to defend all that is holy;
Guard me then O Holy Spirit that I always may be holy.

Reading: John 19:16-28

Then he handed him over to them to be crucified. So they took Jesus, and carrying the cross himself he went out to what is called the Place of the Skull, in Hebrew, Golgotha. There they crucified him, and with him two others, one on either side, with Jesus in the middle. Pilate also had an inscription written and put on the cross. It read, "Jesus the Nazorean, the King of the Jews."

Now many of the Jews read this inscription, because the place where Jesus was crucified was near the city; and it was written in Hebrew, Latin, and Greek. So the chief priests of the Jews said to Pilate, "Do not write 'The King of the Jews,' but that he said, 'I am the King of the Jews.'" Pilate answered, "What I have written, I have written."

When the soldiers had crucified Jesus, they took his clothes and divided them into four shares, a share for each soldier. They also took his tunic, but the tunic was seamless, woven in one piece from the top down. So they said to one another, "Let's not tear it, but cast lots for it to see whose it will be," in order that the passage of scripture might be fulfilled (that says):

They divided my garments among them, and for my vesture they cast lots.

This is what the soldiers did.

Standing by the cross of Jesus were his mother and his mother's sister, Mary the wife of Clopas, and Mary of Magdala. When Jesus saw his mother and the disciple there whom he loved, he said to his mother,

Woman, behold, your son.

Then he said to the disciple,

Behold, your mother.

And from that hour the disciple took her into his home.

After this, aware that everything was now finished, in order that the scripture might be fulfilled, Jesus said,

I thirst.

Commentary

The statements of dying persons tend to voice their important insights and final messages. In his last moments Jesus gives His Mother to all the world in the person of John. Then He "realizes everything was complete." Mary is His last blessing for us. He leaves her to instruct and pray for the Church which is being born out of His side on Calvary. Mary continues to echo, "Let it be done with me as you say."

Reflection

St. Maximilian was always interested in science. He applied one principle of Newtonian physics to his theology: bodies affect each other through a process of action and reaction. Every grace (God's action) reaches us through Christ, the Holy Spirit, and the Immaculata. Our human response (the reaction) passes in reverse order through the Immaculata, the Holy Spirit, and Christ, whether we are aware of it or not. (Through total consecration we acknowledge this fact.)

Some believers have difficulty in understanding Mary's mediation because the Bible mentions only one mediator, Christ. As we examine the double mystery of Jesus and Mary in redemption we can use this formulation to make it clear: our spiritual journey to the Father is not so much a way of going from Mary to Jesus to the Father, but a way of going to Jesus *with* Mary to reach the Father.

It was Jesus' choice to associate his Mother with salvation; it is our choice to accept this association or fail to penetrate the "heartland" of theology. Even now Mary continues her concern to accompany us on the way of salvation; the easiest means of reaching the kingdom of heaven is to join Mary and to introduce her to others. She repays even the smallest reverence to her a hundredfold.

The Words of St. Maximilian
("During her Earthly Life." Taken from an undated manuscript for a book planned on Mary.)

And, so one day, the hour had come for her appearance in this world. She was born into this world in an unknown, hidden and poor home in a Palestinian village. Even the books of Scripture say little about her. We see her in the Scripture at the Annunciation, that moment when she became the Mother of God. We follow her journey to Bethlehem and there we marvel at the advent of God Made Man in a humble stable. Once again, full of concern, we see her on the way to Egypt, consider the difficulties of that voluntary exile, and finally the return to Palestine. We take note, too, of the careful search for the Child Jesus and his finding in the Temple at Jerusalem. Once again at the side of her Son, we find her in Cana of Galilee at the wedding feast, where, for the benefit of the newly married couple the Lord works his first miracle. Jesus goes out to preach and teach; she remains in her little home, worried about the fate that will be his. Mary appears again to accompany Jesus on his journey to Calvary and to the Cross and there, on Golgotha, she is near him at the hour of his death. It is she who holds close to her heart the wounded Body taken down from the Cross. We see her still again when the Holy Spirit is poured out upon her and the Apostles in the Upper Room, as she remains with the followers of her Son as a loving and good Mother, seeing to their preparation. Long decades pass before we can think of her passage into heaven. Though documents may be lacking for many of these years, we know that she spent many years at the side of the Beloved Disciple John.

Sub Tuum Praesidium Prayer

We fly to thy patronage, O holy Mother of God; despise not our petitions in our necessities, but deliver us always from all dangers, O glorious and blessed Virgin. Amen.

Miraculous Medal Prayer

O Mary, conceived without sin, pray for us who have recourse to you, and for all who do not have recourse to you, especially the enemies of the Church and all those recommended to you.

A Chronology of St. Maximilian Kolbe, OFM CONV.

1894, Jan. 8: Raymond Kolbe is **born** in Zdunska Wola, Poland, and is baptized at Assumption Parish.

1902, June 29: Raymond receives his first Holy **Communion** in St. Matthew's Church in Pabianice.

1907: After having heard a Conventual Franciscan preacher in Pabianice, Raymond and his brother, Francis, enter the Order's high-school **seminary** at Lwow.

1910, Sept. 4: Raymond enters the **novitiate** and is given the name Maximilian, and professes his first vows one year later.

1912, Nov. 12: Friar Maximilian begins his **philosophy** curriculum at the Gregorian University in Rome.

1914, Nov. 1: He makes his **final profession** of poverty, chastity and obedience in Rome at the Order's international seminary.

1915, Oct. 22: Despite World War I, his studies continue and he receives the doctorate in philosophy and begins his **theology** curriculum at the Order's major seminary.

1917, Jan. 20: On the seventy-fifth anniversary of Mary's appearance to **Alphonse Ratisbonne**, Friar Maximilian is inspired to found a Marian society.

1917, Oct. 16: With six fellow friars the **Militia of the Immaculata movement is founded** as Mary's instrument to combat the hostility of Freemasonry and other enemies of the Church, and to evangelize the whole world.

1918, April 28: Friar Maximilian is **ordained** to the priesthood in the Church of Sant' Andrea della Valle in Rome. The next day he celebrates his First Mass in the Church of Sant' Andrea della Fratte at the altar where our Lady had appeared to Ratisbonne in 1842.

1919, March 28: The MI is blessed by Pope Benedict XV.

1919, April 4: Fr. Dominic Tavani, Vicar General of the Order, confirms the MI in writing.

1919, July 22: Father Maximilian receives the **doctorate** in theology from the Pontifical Faculty of St. Bonaventure in Rome.

1919, July 23: He sets out for his native land and subsequently in the fall begins teaching Church history in the Order's seminary in Krakow.

1920, Aug. 11: He begins treatment at **Zakopane** for tuberculosis—to be repeated during the ensuing years—although prognosis for his recovery is poor.

1922, Jan. 2: The Vicar of Rome, Cardinal Pompilii, approves the MI as a "**pious union**."

1922, Jan: The first issue, 5,000 copies, of the ***Rycerz Niepokalanow*** (*Knight of the Immaculata*) is printed in Krakow. The editorial office is later moved to Grodno and publication continues there on a obsolete manual press, but the *Rycerz* continues to expand. Meanwhile the infection of tuberculosis is aggravated by his labors.

1926, Dec. 18: Pope Pius XI grants indulgences to the MI in Rome, where the international college of the Order is juridically established as the Primary Center.

1927, July 11: Father Maximilian contacts Prince Drucki-Lubecki to obtain land for a friary and printery. Three months later the construction of **Niepokalanow** (City of the Immaculata) is begun. The religious family consists of two priests and eighteen brothers. In the next twelve years it would grow to about seven hundred members, active in many ministries and operating the largest printing establishment in Central Europe.

1930, Feb. 26: Father Maximilian and four brothers set out for **Nagasaki**, Japan. Two months later the bishop permits them to publish a Marian magazine.

1930, May 24: The first issue, 10,000 copies, of the Japanese *Seibo no Kishi* (*Knight of the Immaculata*) is distributed. Meanwhile Father Maximilian also teaches philosophy at the Nagasaki seminary. The next year a friary and printery, **Mugenzai no Sono** (Garden of the Immaculata), is established on the outskirts of the city. The community grows so that a high-school seminary will be founded six years later.

1936, July 13: Father Maximilian is back in Poland for the third time to participate in a provincial chapter and is chosen superior of Niepokalanow.

1936, Dec. 8: Through his influence the whole Order is consecrated to Mary.

1937, Jan. 19: Father Maximilian leaves for Italy to reorganize the MI in several cities there.

1938, Dec. 8: The first shortwave radio transmissions from Niepokalanow are initiated. Books and periodicals are being published in several languages. Catholic films are in the planning stages.

1939, Sept. 1: World War II begins in Poland. Father Maximilian and other friars are arrested by the Nazis and interned for three months. They are released on December 8.

1940, Nov. 20: The Nazi authorities give permission for one, final issue of the *Rycerz* of 120,000 copies.

1941, Feb. 17: Father Maximilian is taken to **Pawiak** prison in Warsaw by the Gestapo.

1941, May 28: He arrives as part of a trainload of prisoners at Oswiecim (**Auschwitz**) concentration camp, and No. 16670 is tattooed on his arm. St. Maximilian continues his pastoral work secretly among the prisoners. As a priest, he is harassed and assigned the worst tasks.

1941, July 28: Fritsch, the commandant, in reprisal for the escape of one prisoner, condemns ten others to **death by starvation**. St. Maximilian steps forward and asks to replace Francis Gajowniczek, a man with a family. The condemned are locked away in a basement cell. Instead of the usual curses, hymns and prayers to our Lady emanate from the cell as the priest prepares them for a happy death.

1941, Aug. 14: The **death of St. Maximilian** and three prisoners occurs when they are injected with a fatal dose of carbolic acid. Their bodies are cremated the next day.

1971, Oct. 17: Pope Paul VI proclaims Fr. Maximilian a **Blessed** of the Church in a ceremony at St. Peter Basilica in Rome.

1982, Oct. 10: Pope John Paul II proclaims Blessed Maximilian a **Saint** of the Church, calling him a "martyr of charity."

1997, Oct. 16: On the eightieth anniversary of the founding of the Militia of the Immaculata, the Holy See, through the Pontifical Council for the Laity, approves the revised International Governing **Statutes of the MI**. It then erects the MI as an international public association of the faithful (see pp. 79-80). This is the most esteemed recognition the Church can bestow upon a lay organization.

Catechism on the Militia of the Immaculata

What Is the Militia of the Immaculata Movement?

The Militia of the Immaculata movement is an international public association of the faithful founded by St. Maximilian Kolbe in 1917. Its mission is to promote a total consecration to the Blessed Virgin Mary for the purpose of spiritual renewal for individuals and society. Its goal is to bring about the reign of the Sacred Heart of Jesus. It is open to Catholic laity, clergy and religious who recognize the mystery of Mary's Immaculate Conception as the focal point of their spirituality, theology and apostolate.

According to St. Maximilian's own definition, the MI is "a global vision of Catholic life under a new form, consisting in the bond of the Immaculata, our universal Mediatrix before Jesus."

Is the Militia of the Immaculata the Same as the "Knights of the Immaculata?"

Yes. In the United States of America the movement used to be called "Knights" of the Immaculata; however "Militia of the Immaculata" is a more direct translation of the Latin name of the movement, *Militia Immaculatae*, and is consistent with the requirement in the International Statutes of the MI that each country use a name for the movement which lends itself to the internationally used abbreviation, "MI".

Nonetheless, we wish to avoid overtones of militarism, because the MI is movement of prayer and peace, although the warfare remains in the spiritual sense against sin and error.

What Does It Mean that the MI Is an "International Public Association"?

An international public association is the most esteemed recognition the Church can bestow upon a lay organization.

By virtue of their baptismal rights, Catholic laity are free to form their own associations. Private associations are praised and recommended by the Church, but are not formally approved. Public associations, on the other hand, are formally established, or "erected," by the Holy See, a bishop's conference or a diocesan bishop.

Through an official decree and explicit ratification of the association's governing statutes, the Church approves the mission of the public association as being in accord with the very mission of the Church herself. It is adopted, so-to-speak, by the Church as a "public juridical person," giving it explicit rights and responsibilities according to canon law. From that point on, the association comes under the direct supervision of the erecting authority and "receives a mission to pursue the ends which it proposes for itself in the name of the Church" (*Code of Canon Law*, no. 313).

This is the case with the MI, when the Holy See, acting through the Pontifical Council for the Laity, elevated the MI from a "primary pious union" to an international public association on October 16, 1997. The MI was established as an "international" public association because of the wide geographical dispersion of its members and the universal scope of its mission. Thus the MI comes under the jurisdiction of the pope himself, through the administration of the Pontifical Council for the Laity.

Why Did St. Maximilian Found the MI?

In 1917 while a seminarian, twenty-three year old Friar Maximilian Kolbe witnessed a hostile anti-Catholic demonstration in Rome by the Freemasons. They boasted, among other things, that Satan would rule in the Vatican. Maximilian was inspired to found an association that would seek their conversion, and the conversion of all who are trapped in heresy or schism.

Earlier that year he had been deeply impressed by the story of the instantaneous conversion by Our Lady's intercession in 1842 of a prominent Jewish agnostic, Alphonse Ratisbonne. Goaded by a Catholic friend into carrying the Miraculous Medal, Ratisbonne did so and Our Lady appeared to him some days later. This incident convinced Maximilian of the tremendous power of Our Lady's intercession in the conversion of others, and her deep desire to bring even the most hardened unbeliever into a relationship with her Son.

These two incidents were the catalysts for the founding of the MI.

What Are the Conditions for Membership in the MI?

According to the original charter:

- First, after sufficient preparation, one consecrates oneself totally to the service of the Immaculata, to be used as her instrument in evangelizing the world.

- Second, one enrolls in the register of members at an official MI center;

- Third, one must wear or carry the Miraculous Medal.
  The charter also recommends reciting a daily petition to Mary, based on the prayer on the Miraculous Medal.

What Is this Daily Prayer?

"O Mary, conceived without sin, pray for us who have recourse to you, and for all who do not have recourse to you, especially the enemies of the Church and all those recommended to you."

What Other Obligations Are There?

Beyond the obvious obligation of fulfilling one's vocation as perfectly as possible as a Catholic, members are encouraged to renew their act of total consecration every day with the prayer St. Maximilian composed. Also, members use all legitimate means that one's particular state in life makes possible to secure the conversion of other souls, especially by propagating the Miraculous Medal.

What Is the Daily Consecration Prayer?

"O Immaculata, Queen and Mother of the Church, I renew my consecration to you for this day and for always, so that you might use me for the coming of the Kingdom of Jesus in the whole world. To this end I offer you all my prayers, actions and sacrifices of this day."

How Is the MI Different from Other Marian Organizations?

All Marian organizations and groups have similarities of course, but each has its own particular charism. The MI is less rigid in the structures demanded, prayers to be recited, and forms of apostolate that are required by some societies, although the MI provides several models and levels of self-investment in evangelization.

How Is the Kolbean Consecration Different from St. Louis de Montfort's?

As a young man St. Maximilian consecrated himself to Mary using the prayer composed by St. Louis de Montfort, the great Marian apostle of the early eighteenth century. Whereas De Montfort's consecration was primarily concerned with personal holiness, St. Maximilian added a strong apostolic outreach.

Through Kolbean consecration and by joining the MI one becomes a member of a Vatican-approved international association dedicated to the conversion and sanctification of the world. One also shares in the prayers of the MI religious communities and has the formational support that comes from being a part of a formal movement of evangelization.

Also, St. Maximilian gave special emphasis to the doctrine of the Immaculate Conception, which had not yet been infallibly defined in De Montfort's day. By deeply meditating upon Mary's self-title at Lourdes, "I am the Immaculate Conception," he developed this doctrine even further. For Maximilian, the Immaculata is the "Spouse of the Holy Spirit" to whom she is permanently and perfectly united. Through her the Holy Spirit acts exclusively. Therefore, through total consecration according to the Kolbean method we join ourselves to Mary as "Mediatrix," or gateway, of all the graces of the Trinity. The MI member becomes "possessed" in the positive sense as the exclusive instrument of the Immaculata, as she is the exclusive instrument of the Holy Spirit.

As St. Maximilian wrote, "You are always the unconditional, unlimited, irrevocable property and possession of the Immaculata. We desire to be limitlessly obsessed with her and possessed by her that through us she may speak and act in the midst of others."

Why Is there Particular Emphasis on Using the Miraculous Medal?

St. Maximilian was moved by the fact that Our Lady

herself revealed the significance of the design on the medal, and its prayer, to St. Catherine Labouré at her convent at Rue du Bac, Paris. On November 27, 1830, Mary said, "Have a medal struck according to this model. Those who wear it, after being blessed, shall receive great graces, especially if they wear it around their neck. Graces will be abundant for those who have confidence."

St. Maximilian called the medal "a first rate weapon of the MI; it is the bullet with which a faithful soldier cuts down the enemy, that is, evil, and thus rescues souls." He wanted MI members to wear it as "an outward sign of total consecration to the Immaculate Virgin."

What Are Our Three Fronts of Action?

The three fronts of action for MI members are:

- Oneself;

- One's surroundings;

- The world.

First of all, an MI member begins his or her active mission by conversion and personal sanctification: the conquest of self for God is the first indispensable act. "As long as we do not rely upon ourselves, we will be able to attain our goal . . . . With God everything; without God, nothing!"

Secondly, an MI member discerns then, in family, among neighbors, at the workplace or wherever God leads, to evangelize by example, good works and disseminating printed material.

Lastly, MI members open their hearts to every person and the entire world, reflecting the ecclesial dimension of the MI. Indeed, the Church is "Mother and Teacher"; we are to offer ourselves as "a living and effective presence for contributing to the growth of the ecclesial community" (*MI International Statutes*, art. 9).

In What Areas Should MI Members Become Active Apostles?

The international statutes (art. 18) recommend that MI members, mindful that through their total consecration they take on a particular missionary dynamism, should become active apostles in:

- The field of evangelization;

- The level of charity;

- The areas of the mass media.

What Are the Degrees of Membership in the MI?

Membership in the MI is ordered in three degrees: MI-1, MI-2 and MI-3. The degrees refer to the way in which an MI member implements the apostolic dimension of total consecration.

- MI-1: Individually and spontaneously, MI's act within the limits of their own inspiration, zeal and prudence. There is no formal organization, but members work as individuals to influence other people and all society. The widest membership of the MI would fall into this classification.

- MI-2: In an association of members, MI's are organized into groups for mutual support and cooperation in apostolic work to recruit and form others in the service of the local parish or diocese. They disseminate information and penetrate other groups with their Marian spirit. Nevertheless this degree of membership is generally not a full-time ministry.

- MI-3: In a total and unconditional way, these MI's serve Mary without limits in community exclusively for the cause of the Immaculata. These include cities of the Immaculate, centers of the MI, Marian houses, male and female institutes and congregations of Kolbean inspiration.

Are There Different Groups within the MI?

There are four special categories of membership for which MI's may qualify: the Knights at the Foot of the Cross (KFC), MI Contemplatives, MI Youth and Young Adults and MI Prison. Depending on their circumstances they may be MI-1, MI-2 or MI-3.

- KFC's are infirm, suffering, disabled or elderly MI members who participate in "sacrificial suffering." They explicitly offer a portion of their daily prayers, sacrifices and difficulties in union with the Immaculata for the goals of the MI and the good of others.

- MI Contemplatives are religious contemplatives within the MI who choose to live the interior life of Our Lady, and to be an explicit sign of Our Lady's hidden contemplative presence in the life of the movement.

- MI Youth and Young Adults is a nationwide movement of Youth ages 13—35 who live their consecration through retreats and evangelization. The website is www.miyouth.org.

- MI Prison are persons who are incarcerated for whatever reason and consecrate themselves to the Blessed Virgin Mary according to St. Maximilian and join the MI.

How Does One Enroll in the MI?

1. Select a day on which to consecrate yourself to Mary, preferably a Marian feast day. On the day of your enrollment recite the MI Prayer of Consecration (page 94), before an image of Our Lady if possible.

2. Mail your enrollment to the MI national center, requesting that your name be recorded in the official MI

register, or you may enroll yourself on-line at www.consecration.com.

It is recommended that you prepare for your consecration by spiritual reading (particularly on Our Lady and the Immaculate Conception), praying the Rosary, Confession, and attending Mass and receiving Communion on the day (or within eight days) of enrollment.

After making your consecration, ask the Immaculata and St. Maximilian to show you how to best serve the Lord from this moment on.

How Is the Plenary Indulgence for Joining the MI Obtained?

A plenary indulgence—the complete remission of temporal punishment due to sin—is granted by the Church for enrollment in the MI, under the usual conditions of receiving such an indulgence. These are: Confession within the eight days preceding your consecration, Mass and Communion on the day of your consecration or the day preceding, and praying at least an Our Father, Hail Mary and Glory Be for the intentions of the Holy Father.

One must also renounce all attachment to sin, and be free of even venial sin (since punishment can only be remitted for sin already forgiven).

Ritual for Consecration to Mary in the Militia of the Immaculata
(Public or Private)

Opening Hymn

1. Immaculate Mary, thy praises we sing,
   Who reigns now in splendor with Jesus our King.
   Ave, Ave, Ave Maria! Ave, Ave Maria!

2. In heaven the blessed thy glory proclaim,
   On earth we thy children invoke thy fair name.
   Ave, Ave, Ave Maria! Ave, Ave Maria!

Rosary

Reading: Revelation 12:1-17

A great sign appeared in the sky, a woman clothed with the sun, with the moon under her feet, and on her head a crown of twelve stars. She was with child and wailed aloud in pain as she labored to give birth. Then another sign appeared in the sky; it was a huge red dragon, with seven heads and ten horns, and on its heads were seven diadems. Its tail swept away a third of the stars in the sky and hurled them down to the earth. Then the dragon stood before the woman about to give birth, to devour her child when she gave birth. She gave birth to a son, a male child, destined to rule all the nations with an iron rod. Her child was caught up to God and his throne. The woman herself fled into the desert where she had a place prepared by God, that there she might be taken care of for twelve hundred and sixty days.

Then war broke out in heaven; Michael and his angels battled against the dragon. The dragon and its angels fought back, but they did not prevail and there was no longer any place for them in heaven. The huge dragon, the ancient serpent, who is called the Devil and Satan, who deceived the whole world, was thrown down to earth, and its angels were thrown down with it.

Then I heard a loud voice in heaven say:

> *Now have salvation and power come, and the kingdom of our God and the authority of his Anointed. For the accuser of our brothers is cast out, who accuses them before our God day and night.*
> *They conquered him by the blood of the Lamb and by the word of their testimony; love for life did not deter them from death.*
> *Therefore, rejoice, you heavens, and you who dwell in them. But woe to you, earth and sea, for the Devil has come down to you in great fury, for he knows he has but a short time.*

When the dragon saw that it had been thrown down to the earth, it pursued the woman who had given birth to the male child. But the woman was given the two wings of the great eagle, so that she could fly to her place in the desert, where, far from the serpent, she was taken care of for a year, two years, and a half-year.

The serpent, however, spewed a torrent of water out of his mouth after the woman to sweep her away with the current. But the earth helped the woman and opened its mouth and swallowed the flood that the dragon spewed out of its mouth. Then the dragon became angry with the woman and went off to wage war against the rest of her offspring, those who keep God's commandments and bear witness to Jesus. It took its position on the sand of the sea.

Reflection/Homily

Some theologians speculate on the fall of Satan. Why did such a perceptive and intelligent creature rebel against God, who was obviously above him? It is said that God presented Lucifer with a vision of the future: a lesser creature of human nature would be joined to divinity itself, and the Mother of that God-Man would be queen over even the angels. Satan recoiled from such submission; this was the beginning of the enmity between her offspring and his. In a Marian prayer the Church says of Mary, "You have destroyed all heresies in the world," which come from Satan, the "father of lies." Before his final Passover, Jesus said, "Now the prince of this world—Satan—is being cast out" (Jn 12:31).

Finally, in the twelfth chapter of Revelation, Mary is said to be the sign of victory over the forces of evil. The war is not over, of course, until Jesus comes again, but Mary in her own person by the power of the Holy Spirit, her Spouse, has escaped sin and error and has become the model of the Church's ultimate victory. In her we see the qualities of ever-youthful vigor yet agelessness. She is the *first* member of the Church to be "immaculate": first in time because she was there at the Christ-event, first in response because of the quality of her commitment to Jesus, first in rank because of her eminent cooperation with the Lord of history, first in honor because all generations have called her "blessed." Even if we are the least in rank and response, nevertheless she will share her victory with us, helping us become "immaculate," worthy to re-enter paradise!

Rite of Consecration

Presider: Dear brothers and sisters, the Lord has inspired you to entrust yourselves wholly to Mary in order to become instruments of his grace in the Militia of the Immaculata for the conversion and sanctification of all mankind. Do you wish, therefore, with the help of the Holy Spirit, to live your lives in perfect union with the Immaculata and to be for all your brothers and sisters a light and an example of Christian life?

All: Yes, I do.

Renewal of Baptismal Promises & Profession of Faith

Presider: The act of total consecration to Our Lady will lead you to live your Baptism fully. For this reason we now renew our baptismal promises.

Do you reject sin, so as to live in the freedom of God's children?

All: I do.

Presider: Do you reject the glamour of evil and refuse to be mastered by sin?

All: I do.

Presider: Do you reject Satan, father and prince of darkness?

All: I do.

Presider: Do you believe in God, the Father Almighty, Creator of heaven and earth?

All: I do.

Presider: Do you believe in Jesus Christ, his only Son, our Lord, who was born of the Virgin Mary, was crucified, died, and was buried, rose from the dead, and is now seated at the right hand of the Father?

All: I do.

Presider: Do you believe in the Holy Spirit, the Holy Catholic Church, the communion of saints, the forgiveness of sins, the resurrection of the body, and life everlasting?

All: I do.

Invitation to Consecration

MI Consecration Prayer for Individuals

All: O Immaculata, Queen of heaven and earth, Refuge of sinners and our most loving Mother, God has willed to entrust the entire order of mercy to you.

I, (name), a repentant sinner, cast myself at your feet humbly imploring you to take me with all that I am and have, wholly to yourself as your possession and property.

Please make of me, of all my powers of soul and body, of my whole life, death and eternity, whatever most pleases you. If it pleases you, use all that I am and have without reserve, wholly to accomplish what was said of you: "She will crush your head," and "You alone have destroyed all heresies in the whole world."

Let me be a fit instrument in your immaculate and merciful hands for introducing and increasing your glory to the maximum in all the many strayed and indifferent souls, and thus help extend as far as possible the blessed kingdom of the most Sacred Heart of Jesus. For wherever you enter you obtain the grace of conversion and growth in holiness, since it is through your hands that all graces come to us from the most Sacred Heart of Jesus.

Presider: Allow me to praise you, O Sacred Virgin.

All: Give me strength against your enemies.

Blessing and Investing with the Miraculous Medal

Presider: Our help is in the name of the Lord.

All: Who made heaven and earth.

Presider: Let us pray:

> Almighty and merciful God, who through the many apparitions of the Immaculate Virgin on earth has deigned to work great wonders, bless + these medals, so that all who wear them in love and veneration might enjoy your protection and gain your mercy. Through Christ our Lord.

All: Amen.

> The new consecrants receive the blessed medal.

Presider: Receive this holy medal, wear it with faith and venerate it with love.

Consecrant: Amen.

After all consecrants have been invested:

Presider: If you do all these things, the Faithful and Immaculate Virgin Mother of God will protect and defend you from all harm in soul and body. As the Immaculate Virgin is ever ready to renew her wondrous acts of kindness, may she obtain for you in her mercy whatever you humbly ask of God, so that both in life and in death you may rest happily in her motherly embrace.

All: Amen.

Final Exhortation

Presider: Let us pray to Our Lady using the prayer recommended for daily recitation by St. Maximilian Kolbe:

All: O Mary, conceived without sin, pray for us who have recourse to you, and for those who do not have recourse to you, especially for the enemies of Holy Church and for all those recommended to you.

Closing Hymn

1. Hail holy queen enthroned above, O Maria.
   Hail mother of mercy and of love, O Maria.
   Triumph all ye cherubim,
   Sing with us ye seraphim.
   Heaven and earth resound the hymn
   Salve, salve, salve regina.

2. Our life, our sweetness here below, O Maria.
   Our hope in sorrow and in woe, O Maria.
   Triumph all ye cherubim
   Sing with us ye seraphim
   Heaven and earth resound the hymn
   Salve, salve, salve regina.